Bob Sakata
American Farmer

Bob Sakata
American Farmer

A NOW YOU KNOW BIO

Number Twelve in the Series

Daniel Blegen

Filter Press, LLC
Palmer Lake, Colorado

To the 120,000 Americans of Japanese heritage whose
country forced them from their homes in 1942.
To the Americans who
defended their country as members of the
442nd Regimental Combat Team.
To the farmers of America who feed the world.

ISBN: 978-0-86541-093-0
Library of Congress Control Number: 2008938508
Copyright © 2009 Daniel Blegen. All Rights Reserved.
Map illustrations on pages 3, 37, and 64 copyright © 2009 Vicki Blegen.
Photographs of Bob Sakata on cover, page vi, and page 91 by Daniel Blegen.

Bob Sakata: American Farmer

Published by
Filter Press, LLC, P.O. Box 95, Palmer Lake, Colorado
719-481-2420 • info@FilterPressBooks.com

Printed in the United States of America

Contents

1   **Roots**

Bob Sakata grows corn. Lots of corn. Twenty-five million ears of corn a year, to be exact.

You have probably eaten Bob's sweet corn. But you had to work for it. First, you tugged away its green husks to find the kernels. They were hiding inside, yellow and plump and in rows like a mouthful of smiling teeth. You plucked off silky strings that stuck to your fingers.

Then you floated the corn in boiling water. Or zapped it in a microwave. Or even better, grilled it on the barbecue.

You ate that ear of warm corn with butter. And a little salt. And its juices ran down your fingers to your elbows.

And if that ear of corn could hear, it would have heard you say, "Mmm, Mmm, Mmm, Mmm, Mmm."

Bob Sakata grows his famous corn on 3,000 **acres** of land north of Denver. Each summer he also grows 20 million pounds of onions and 20 million pounds of cabbage. He sells his produce in grocery stores throughout Colorado and as far away as Texas. For over 60 years Bob Sakata has been one of the most successful farmers in the United States. Bob works hard. He works creatively and shares his skills with others.

But Bob's success did not come easily. As a child in California he lived in poverty. During World War II, the government forced Bob and 120,000 other Japanese Americans to leave their homes. He had to live like a prisoner in the Utah desert, just because he was Japanese American.

Bob Sakata credits much of his success to his father, Mantaro, who was born in 1884 in Japan. As a boy, Mantaro was already a farmer. "His family had a couple of hectares of fruit trees," Bob said, about 2.5 acres. Their orchard was no bigger than a school playground. Bob Sakata's story begins in Japan.

Mantaro Sakata lived on Japan's small southern island, Kyushu (KYOO SHOO). He and his brothers

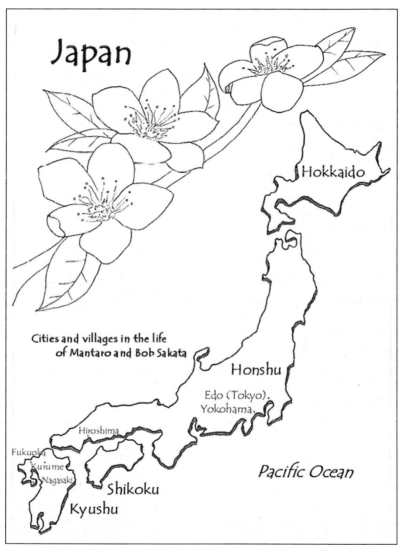

Japan

Hokkaido

Cities and villages in the life
of Mantaro and Bob Sakata

Honshu

Edo (Tokyo).
Yokohama.

Hiroshima

Fukuoka
Kurume
Nagasaki

Shikoku
Kyushu

Pacific Ocean

*Mantaro Sakata was born in 1884 near the village of Kurume
on the island of Kyushu in southern Japan.*

farmed near the tiny village of Kurume (KOO ROO MAY). He spent long days tending plum, apricot, and cherry trees. If a tree was dying, Bob said, Mantaro grafted a branch from it onto a healthy tree. Grafting is attaching a shoot from one tree onto the trunk of another. A grafted shoot takes the life-giving sap from its new parent and becomes part of it. "Dad was a pro at grafting trees," Bob said.

Mantaro Sakata could even graft a shoot onto a tree of a totally different kind. He once grafted a plum tree shoot to a walnut tree. The shoot grew healthy and produced plums. The branches of the parent tree still produced walnuts. "I wish I had learned how to do that," Bob said.

Mantaro also had to do the lowliest farm work in all of Japan.

On Kyushu, there was little land to grow crops. Yet the farmers had to feed the island's people. They had to farm creatively. "They wouldn't waste an acre of land," Bob said. "They used to grow vegetables in the paths between the rows of trees." Those paths would have been a waste of precious land if not used.

All summer Mantaro pulled weeds that tried to choke the vegetables. He scared off birds that ate more

Bob Sakata's father, Mantaro, carried on a Japanese farming tradition as he tended the family orchard. This print by the Japanese artist Keibun Matsumara (1779–1843) shows a bird perched on the branch of a fruit tree.

than their share of plums and apricots and cherries. He carried bucketsful of water to the crops when the rains failed. In the fall he harvested the fruits and vegetables.

Growing vegetables was not considered the lowliest farm work.

Another of Mantaro's jobs was carrying the honey bucket. It was not a sweet job. Even the name "honey bucket" was a joke. The "honey" carried in the bucket was human waste and urine. The waste was used as a

fertilizer for the crops. Carrying the honey bucket definitely was the lowliest work in Japan.

Gathering human waste was nasty work, of course. But Japanese farmers had been using this smelly resource for hundreds of years. In the late 1800s, farmers gathered human waste from the growing cities like nearby Fukuoka (FOE koe OH ka). There were two practical benefits of recycling human waste. Recycling kept the city's water supply from being polluted. It also gave farmers a needed raw material. Crops take nutrients from the soil. Without nutrients, the soil will not support growth. The soil had to be fertilized every year.

Carrying the honey bucket was a lowly job. But for the Japanese people it was a necessary job. It was as necessary as collecting trash and recycling are today. When the waste was mixed with leaves and plant stalks, it formed rich compost. Nothing was wasted in Japan. The "honey bucket" made farming there possible.

Mantaro Sakata worked hard, and yet he was poor. American children are told that they can become anything they want, even president. A Japanese child could not even dream of becoming the emperor of Japan. To become emperor, one had to be born into the royal family. During Mantaro's childhood the emperor of

Japan was the Emperor Taishÿ. Mantaro considered him a god. All Japanese citizens considered the emperor a god. He was far from his people, never seen and never heard.

A class system kept most dreams from coming true for young people. Even after Japan did away with the class system, stumbling blocks remained. Farmers on Kyushu earned little income and paid many taxes. A poor boy grew up to be a poor man. No matter how hard he worked, Mantaro Sakata would carry the "honey bucket" for the rest of his life.

Mantaro's one hope was to leave Japan for a country offering him opportunities. A California businessman gave him that chance. "There was an **entrepreneur**," said Bob Sakata, "who bought land in California. He decided he wanted to grow rice in the San Francisco Bay area." The man was not a farmer, but he knew that rice was Japan's most important crop. "He went to Japan looking for people to help him," Bob said. "My father was one of those people." Mantaro's creativity caught the businessman's attention.

However, people from Japan were not totally free to settle in the United States. The businessman had to ask the government for permission to bring workers here.

Mantaro Sakata's creativity and knowledge of rice farming in Japan helped him come to America in 1902.

This Japanese woodcut from the late nineteenth century shows travelers walking along the path through a rice paddy with Mount Fuji in the background.

He got that permission in Washington. In 1902 Mantaro Sakata left his family in Japan.

Mantaro crossed the Pacific Ocean on a ship named the *S. S. Doric*. It ran on steam power but was still rigged with masts like older sailing ships. *The Doric* left Japan on June 18, 1902. A clerk questioned the ship's passengers as they boarded. He wrote information about them in the ship's official manifest. It says that Mantaro Sakata was 18 years old when he boarded at Yokohama, Japan. He was not married but could read and write and had paid for the voyage himself. Under the manifest column asking for "Calling or Occupation," the clerk wrote the word "farmer."

Mantaro Sakata may not have been traveling alone. His name appears with those of three other young men from Kyushu. Genzo Narahashi, 17, was a student. Yataro Narahashi, possibly his brother, was a 21-year-old farmer. Gisaburo Akiyama, 25, was also a farmer. Maybe they were recruited as a team to grow rice in California. Whether they knew each other or not, they were not wealthy travelers. A final question asked by the ship's clerk was: "Are you in possession of money?" Mantaro answered, "$30." That was not much money to start a whole new life.

Fifteen days later Mantaro and the others arrived at San Francisco in "the land of the free." It was the 5th of July. They had missed America's 4th of July birthday celebration by one day. How did Mantaro feel about his ocean voyage? What fears did he have about living in a huge, new country? How would he talk with people who could not understand his language? The ship's manifest gives no answers. Yet Mantaro must have felt himself a fortunate man indeed. He had come to a country where he could create his own future.

There is no record of what Mantaro did when he arrived in San Francisco. He may have worked a variety of jobs before the rice farm was begun. But it is known that the road to his future was rocked four years later. In 1906 a huge earthquake struck San Francisco. The earthquake destroyed the city's entire downtown. An enormous fire followed. It did even more damage to the rest of the city. The San Francisco earthquake and fire killed 700 people. It destroyed 400 million dollars worth of property. Homes, shops, and office buildings were turned into piles of rubble.

The father of writer Yoshiko Uchida **emigrated** from Japan in 1906. His ship docked in San Francisco three months after the earthquake. Yoshiko wrote that

Market Street in San Francisco in 1906 is shown
before the earthquake and fire.

The same street is shown after the San Francisco Earthquake
ruined buildings and left piles of rubble.

Two men are cleaning up the street in front of buildings damaged by the San Francisco Earthquake in 1906.

Library of Congress, Prints & Photographs Division, LC-USZ62-98494

her father saw "the ferry building still askew and Market Street piled high with ash." Japanese and Chinese **immigrants** were recruited to clean up the city. Mantaro Sakata was one of them.

He certainly would have worked hard on the cleanup. The mountains of rubble had to be moved one shovelful at a time. After the San Francisco earthquake, plans for the rice farm were abandoned. Mantaro Sakata would have to look for other work. He was alone and far from his village of Kurume, Japan.

2   Sprouts

Many Japanese immigrants worked on farms in the valleys east of San Francisco Bay. Mantaro did, too. "Dad did gardening work of all kinds," Bob Sakata said, "near Centerville, which is now called Fremont." Then he became the personal gardener for a man named George Emmanuel. He cared for Mr. Emmanuel's lawns and flower beds. "On top of that," Bob said, "he had the responsibility of taking care of an orchard." Mantaro must have felt right at home. He was tending apricot and cherry trees again.

"Dad wanted to be on his own, but he didn't have any money to buy his own place," Bob said. In the early 1900s the United States did not even allow Japanese immigrants to own land. George Emmanuel helped Mantaro toward his goal. He was the first of many individuals who stepped up for the Sakatas. "Mr. Emmanuel saw the talent in Dad," Bob said. He established Mantaro as a sharecropper on ten acres of his land that included an orchard. A sharecropper grows crops and then pays the landowner a share of his profits.

Mantaro gained more independence when George Emmanuel began renting the land to him. Mantaro grew all kinds of vegetables on those ten acres. "You name it, he grew it," Bob said. Because of the mild weather in the San Francisco Bay area, Mantaro could grow crops all year long, not just in the summer.

Mantaro Sakata was here to stay, and he was ready to get married. But few Japanese women lived here. And in Japan a man's wife was chosen for him. The **elders** of the village chose his bride. It was the custom. Often a man did not even know the woman chosen for him. When Mantaro decided to marry, he followed the custom. He sent a letter to the village elders in Kurume. He asked them to find a wife.

In the letter he probably described his farm in California. He probably wrote that he was not lazy or afraid of work. He could provide a good living. And with the letter he probably sent a picture of himself. Many weeks later, he received a letter in return. It was from the young woman chosen for him by the elders. She too enclosed a picture. This is how the Japanese immigrants met their brides. The young brides then made the voyage to the United States. They were called the picture brides.

Mantaro paid for his picture bride's voyage. He met her for the first time when her ship docked in San Francisco. They were married soon afterwards. "My mother came as a picture bride in about 1920," Bob said. "Her name was Aki."

Mantaro followed the Japanese marriage customs. He did not think of them as unusual, as we might today. Many years later Mantaro joked with his son Bob about marriage. "You folks in the United States fall in love and then get married," Mantaro said, "and then you have all kinds of divorces. We [Japanese] get married and then fall in love. And it sticks."

The mother of writer Yoshiko Uchida also came to California as a picture bride. Yoshiko wrote with pride about how her trusting mother left Japan. In her book, *Desert Exile,* Yoshiko wrote:

It seems incredible to me that my mother... could have taken so enormous a leap across the

Pacific Ocean, leaving behind her family and friends and all that was dear to her… [The picture brides] came to an alien land, created homes for their men, worked beside them in fields, small shops, and businesses, and at the same time bore most of the responsibility for raising their children. Theirs was a determination and endurance born…of an uncommon spirit.

Mantaro Sakata's picture bride, Aki, made the same enormous leap of faith across the ocean. She too possessed an "uncommon spirit."

The marriage of Mantaro and Aki did "stick." They worked their farm together and started a family. Their first child was named Harry. He was followed a year later by twin girls, Mitsuko and Fusako, who were usually called by their nicknames, Mitsie and Fusi. Bob was Mantaro's and Aki's youngest child. Bob Sakata was born in San Jose, California, on April 15, 1926.

Bob grew up working on the leased land near Centerville. A few miles to the west lay the beautiful San Francisco Bay. To the north was the city of San Francisco, where the Golden Gate Bridge was completed in 1937. That famous bridge still forms a

Photograph courtesy of Bob Sakata

Mantaro Sakata is shown with his "picture bride" Aki Nishimura near the time of their marriage in 1920.

The Sakatas posed for this family photogragh in 1931. From left to right:
Aki, Mantaro, Mitsie, Fusi, Harry and Bob. Though they were poor, their formal
clothing shows the pride they took in themselves. The girls are wearing
traditional Japanese kimonos.

gateway to the Pacific. To the east of the Sakata farm were green, rolling hills.

Mantaro Sakata's farm was tiny compared to the 3,000 acres of land that his son Bob owns today in Colorado. Farming in the early 1900s was still done by hand. Ten acres was all one farm family could manage. The Sakatas raised a variety of vegetables and tended their small orchard. They had to plant, weed, and hoe by hand just as Mantaro had done back in Japan. They were also just as "dirt poor" as Mantaro had been there.

When Bob was a child, the Sakatas lived in a plain, wood frame house with only four rooms. At the front of the house was a parlor. Today we would call it a living room. There was a kitchen, and there were two bedrooms, one for the parents and one for all four kids.

Despite their poverty, the Sakatas maintained a tremendous amount of pride in themselves. "Our kitchen had a dirt floor," Bob said, "but Mother kept it so clean you could eat off it." He also remembered that his mother kept old newspapers. She glued the newspapers to the walls of the kids' bedroom with a rice paste. She could not afford real wallpaper. The *San Francisco Examiner* and *Oakland Tribune* were not the fanciest wall coverings, but they kept some of the wind from blowing through the cracks. "We grew up in real poverty," Bob said, then added, "but we didn't realize it until we were invited to visit our friends' homes."

Later, the Sakatas built a traditional Japanese bath house. It had a large, round tub, something like a hot tub. The water was heated by a fire built beneath it.

When Bob was a child, his father and mother still spoke Japanese. "My father had no education higher than elementary school, but he had common sense,"

Bob said. His parents learned enough English to shop in town and to conduct business. Bob grew up speaking both Japanese and English. He is still **bilingual** today. He said, "I have to hand it to my father and mother. They told all of us kids, 'You're going to go to American schools and you study and learn how to speak English. But at home we want to teach you how to speak Japanese.' " Speaking his parents' native Japanese was most helpful for Bob as an adult. He was asked to visit Japan as a consultant to the Mitsubishi Corporation. With only a bit of review, he was able to conduct business there without needing a Japanese **interpreter**.

Bob clearly recalls the year he was in kindergarten, 1932. A friend of his family came to the school one day and asked that Bob and his brother and sisters be excused from class. Their mother was very sick, the friend said, and the kids must go to see her. Their mother, Aki, had caught a bad cold that had worsened into **pneumonia**, a serious lung disease. She was in a hospital in San Jose where she died later that day. "Mother would be alive today," Bob said, "if they had only had **penicillin** then." Penicillin is an **antibiotic** now used to fight infections like pneumonia, but it was not available in a usable form until 1940, just a few years after Aki Sakata's death. Penicillin was looked on as a wonder drug. It saved the lives of countless soldiers during World War II, which began for the United States in 1941.

After Aki's death, Bob's twin sisters, Mitsie and Fusi, took on their mother's duties. "They became my mother," Bob said, who was just six years old when his mother died. His sisters were not much older. They were only 11. Mantaro Sakata also faced a whole new challenge. He had to do the hard work of farming while raising four children as a single parent. Bob respects his father's determination to do the right thing for his kids. Bob said that his father "would go to work in the fields at 3:00 or 4:00 in the morning, well before daylight. But he would always come back to the house at 7:00 to see that we kids had something to eat before going to school." Sometimes that meant only rice and tea or pickled vegetables. But Mantaro Sakata always made sure that his children were ready for the day.

3   Growth

"I guess I was kind of a lazy kid," Bob said. "I was always looking for ways to get things done easier. I was blessed with a very curious mind." Bob's desire to make his chores easier was a sign of creativity. Creativity can make anyone's work more effective. For example, a farmer who can harvest crops faster can make a better living for his family.

As a boy Bob did not read comic books before going to sleep at night as other boys did. "I would enjoy reading tractor magazines and equipment magazines," he said. "I'd look at them and I would say 'There must be a better way than the way they're making things.' "

His "laziness" first sparked his creativity when he was just ten years old. One of Bob's summer chores was harvesting corn. It is the crop that Bob is famous for today. Bob's dad walked the rows of corn, picking ears as he went. Bob followed, collecting the ears in a bushel basket. As the basket filled, it became heavier and heavier. Too heavy, Bob thought. Too heavy to carry to the end of each long row where he would empty it in the shade of the orchard. The August sun was hot. The razor-sharp leaves of the stalks cut his sweaty face. His skin was stinging. He was probably wearing work boots that did not fit quite right. They were hand-me-downs from his older brother Harry. Imagine Bob complaining, "I'm getting tired. I can't carry this darn heavy basket another step."

So he used his creativity. But not to come up with an excuse to get out of the work. Bob used his creativity to do his work more effectively. He built a wagon that was narrow enough to pull between the corn rows. He topped the wagon with a box of wood slats. The box would hold the corn, much more corn than Bob could carry in a basket. That made his work more effective. But he did not stop there. Next he rigged the wagon to be pulled by a horse. So instead of carrying a heavy basket all day, Bob was simply guiding a horse. "The horse did all the work," Bob pointed out.

Since the wagon box held more corn than a basket, it did not have to be unloaded as often, either. The harvesting was done with far less sweat and strain for the creative farm boy. It was also done in far less time for his busy farmer father. Mantaro must have been proud of his son.

Bob Sakata grew up during the 1930s. It was a decade of terrible money problems for the entire country. Many people lost their jobs. Families had to get along with less income than they were used to. Those years are now called The Great Depression. It was only "great" because of its huge, negative impact on Americans. Fortunately for farmers, city folks still had to buy food. The Sakatas made enough income from farming to live on. When Bob's brother Harry turned 16, he got his drivers license. He drove their Model T Ford truck to the Oakland Farmers Market. At the market, he sold the Sakata's fruits and vegetables to grocery stores and restaurants.

Yet, his family's poverty was painfully clear to Bob. "When I started high school, the bus would pick me up. I had about a quarter mile to walk to the road," Bob said. "But I would go a little early and...stand in front of a better looking house." He hoped the kids on the bus would not notice the tiny house he came from. He was embarrassed by his family's poverty. Visiting the homes of both Japanese and Anglo friends made him even more aware of it.

In high school Bob again showed his willingness to work hard and creatively. He knew that the key to success is education. "I chose to take seven solid subjects each semester so that I could graduate in just two years," he said. Solids are the core subjects. They are the basis of a good education. Solids are classes like math, science, history, and English.

For some teenagers at Washington High School in Fremont, California, the high school years probably seemed to drag on forever. Some could not wait to graduate. Getting out of school may have been part of Bob's thinking. But choosing to graduate in two years meant that he was willing to study harder than other students. He was willing to do more homework. Each day at school, Bob's first class started at 8 A.M. His last class started at 4 P.M. And Bob still had to help his dad with the farm chores. He also found time to become a member of the Future Farmers of America (FFA). The teacher who sponsored the FFA club saw Bob's talent. He would also play an important role in Bob's future.

After two years of high school, Bob could have farmed full time like his dad. Surprisingly, that was not his plan. "A farmer is the last thing I wanted to be," Bob emphasized. He was thinking into his future. He wanted more education. However, during his second year in high school, explosive world events took Bob Sakata on an unplanned detour.

Big events in other parts of the world sometimes affect us personally. It does not matter how far away those events may be. Recent events that have touched Americans include the terrorist attacks on New York City on September 11, 2001 and the following war in Iraq. In 1941 Bob Sakata was a 15-year-old sophomore in high school. World events totally disrupted his life.

Huge changes had taken place in Japan since 1902 when Mantaro Sakata left his homeland. Japan had become a modern nation. It had built factories and a powerful military force. To support the changes, Japan had to find coal to power its factories. It had to find oil to fuel its military ships and tanks. Japan did not have enough of these resources.

The political and military leaders of Japan wanted to attack nearby countries to take their resources.

Japan's Shÿwa Emperor agreed with their decisions. Japan first invaded China with a series of brutal attacks in the 1930s. Meanwhile in Europe, Nazi Germany — led by Adolph Hitler — was invading its neighbor countries.

Then on December 7, 1941, the Japanese Air Force made a surprise attack on the United States Navy at Pearl Harbor, Hawaii. Japan attacked the United States at Pearl Harbor as part of its plan to steal

Library of Congress, Prints & Photographs Division, LC-USW33-018433-C

Smoke billows from the battleship USS West Virginia as sailors on a small boat attempt to rescue a seaman during the Japanese attack on Pearl Harbor.

President Franklin D. Roosevelt signed a Declaration of War against Japan and Germany after the Japanese attack on Pearl Harbor on December 7, 1941.

the energy resources. Most of the ships of the United States Navy in the Pacific were docked there. The Japanese Air Force destroyed eight U.S. battleships, nine cruisers, and many smaller ships. Even worse, Japanese airmen killed 2,403 Americans stationed on those ships. One day after the attack, President Franklin Roosevelt asked Congress to declare war against Japan. Suddenly the United States was preparing to fight a full-scale war against the powerful Japanese forces. Congress also declared war against Germany and Italy to help the countries that were under attack in Europe.

The Pearl Harbor attack shocked America. The war that followed brought hardships to every family. It brought a unique set of hardships to the Sakatas and the other 120,000 Japanese Americans living here. The war would uproot them from their homes. The Sakata family would be forced off of their farm.

4 Uprooted

L
ike most other immigrants, Bob Sakata's parents had come to the United States for the freedom to lead better lives. The first Japanese immigrants had settled in California, Oregon, and Washington early in the 1800s. Later some settled farther inland. In Colorado, for example, Japanese immigrants first settled in the 1870s. Still, there were very few Japanese immigrants in the United States in 1940. The federal census showed only 47,305 Japanese-born immigrants. Most lived in California, where they made up only one percent of that state's population. The number of Japanese living in the United States was small partly because the government had made it difficult for Asians to settle here. The Oriental Exclusion Act of 1907 even barred Asian immigrants from becoming citizens. This law was not abolished

until after World War II, in 1952.

Like Mantaro Sakata, most Japanese immigrants chose to live in and around the cities of San Francisco, Los Angeles, and Seattle. The immigrants who had moved here from Japan called themselves the *issei* (EES say). *Issei* is a Japanese word meaning first generation. The word indicates that the Japanese immigrants thought of themselves as permanent residents, the first generation of many who would live here.

The 1940 census also recorded that there were an additional 79,642 American-born Japanese Americans in this country. They are called the *nisei* (KNEE say), the second generation. Under United States law, anyone born here becomes a citizen at birth. So the *nisei*, the second generation Japanese, were all United States citizens. As a group the *issei* and their *nisei* children were notably hard working. They took up jobs in farming, shop keeping, and business. They valued education, family unity, fairness, and personal responsibility. In other words, they embraced the ideals of America. Though they thought fondly of their homeland, they were now proud and loyal Americans.

On that Sunday in December, 1941, when Pearl Harbor was attacked, Bob Sakata was in a hospital in

San Jose, California. He was recovering from routine surgery to remove his tonsils. Like most other Americans, Bob probably heard about the attack in a news bulletin announced on the radio. However, he had no idea that the attack would change his entire life.

The attack by the country of Japan made Americans suspicious and fearful of the Japanese Americans living on the West Coast. Many Americans no longer saw the *issei* and their *nisei* children clearly. Instead of seeing hard working, loyal immigrant neighbors who just happened to be Japanese, many began seeing "the enemy." What Americans feared most was that the Japanese Americans would some-how help the Japanese military attack the West Coast. The suspicions and fears turned to hatred and **discrimination** against the Japanese Americans.

Bob Sakata, however, said he was never discriminated against at his California high school, either by his teachers or his Anglo classmates. Other Japanese Americans did feel hatred sting. In the nearby town of Berkeley, Yoshiko Uchida and her friends were suddenly excluded by their Anglo classmates. Some Anglo-owned stores even refused to serve her. Maybe most painful for Yoshiko was the question asked her by one of her close Anglo friends. "Did you have any idea that the Pearl Harbor attack was coming?" the friend asked bluntly. She spoke as if Yoshiko and her girlfriends might actually have been involved.

Historian William Manchester has also recorded incidents of unfair treatment against Japanese Americans. "Milkmen refused to deliver their milk," he wrote. "Grocers wouldn't sell them food." Today Bob Sakata feels no anger toward the Americans who practiced these forms of racial discrimination. He does, however, hold newspaper writers responsible for stirring up hatred. Newspapers began to use nasty words to describe his people. One **columnist** even wrote, "Personally I hate the Japanese, and that goes for all of them." He gave his opinion that the Japanese Americans were too dangerous to live in our cities and in our countryside. He called for the government to send them all to prison camps in desert areas of the West. Some government officials in Washington agreed with the columnist's hateful opinions.

Historians now know that the State Department had told President Roosevelt that the Japanese Americans showed "a remarkable, even extraordinary degree of loyalty" to the United States. But President Roosevelt believed the hateful and untrue accusations instead. Two months after the Pearl Harbor attack, he issued Executive Order 9066. The order told the United States secretary of war to remove both "**aliens and non-aliens**" from parts of the country where they might pose a military danger. That meant that all Japanese Americans would be forced out of California, Oregon, and Washington. Government officials reasoned that the Japanese would attack the West Coast next. The officials also reasoned — incorrectly — that Japanese Americans living in those states might help the Japanese military plan an attack.

Executive Order 9066 did not actually include the words "Japanese Americans," but it was clear that the order was aimed at them. The word "aliens" in the order referred to the Japan-born *issei*, many of whom were not citizens. The word "non-aliens" meant the *nisei*, who were American citizens by birth.

The United States was also preparing to go to war against Germany and Italy in Europe. But there was no similar executive order against German American or Italian American citizens. Those groups were a much larger percentage of the American population.

Historians estimate that in 1940 Americans of German ancestry made up between 30 percent and 35 percent of the country's population. During the same year, Japanese Americans made up only one percent of the population of California. But the large percentage of the country's population that was German American was not considered a threat, even though the United States was also at war with Germany. The German Americans, however, were Anglo, not Asian.

Executive Order 9066 was issued by President Roosevelt on February 19, 1942. About 10,000 Japanese Americans left the West Coast states during a "voluntary **evacuation**" period. They moved inland to states such as Colorado and Utah. By March, the government had plans to remove the remaining 110,000. The Japanese Americans were told to get rid of their possessions, including their houses and cars. They were to be rounded up by Army and National Guard troops and sent to "relocation camps."

Historian William Manchester and others have called Executive Order 9066 "a national disgrace."

5 Transplanted

Fear and **prejudice** had prompted Executive Order 9066. In April of 1942, government officials notified the Japanese Americans on the West Coast. The time had come to leave their homes. They would be taken to temporary assembly centers and held as prisoners. Meanwhile, more permanent relocation camps were being built in isolated areas in Arizona, Arkansas, California, Colorado, Idaho, Montana, and Utah. The government would transfer the Japanese Americans to those isolated camps. They would be kept locked up until the war with Japan ended. Mantaro Sakata and his children were about to lose their freedom.

Almost overnight, government posters appeared in the neighborhoods and small towns where Japanese Americans lived. Bob Sakata may have seen one as he

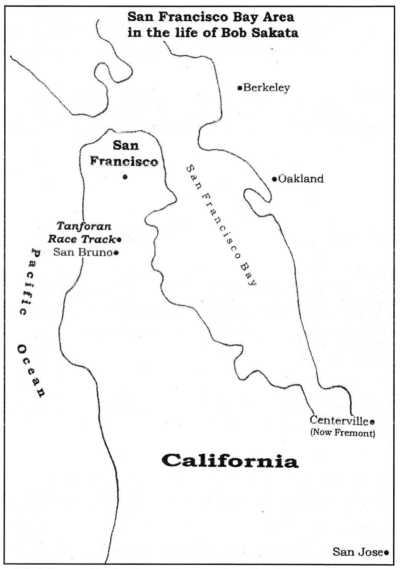

**San Francisco Bay Area
in the life of Bob Sakata**

•Berkeley

**San
Francisco**
•

San Francisco Bay

•Oakland

*Tanforan
Race Track*•
San Bruno•

Pacific

Ocean

Centerville•
(Now Fremont)

California

San Jose•

*Bob Sakata and his family were forced to leave their home and possessions
near Centerville, California. They were taken to an assembly center on the
grounds of Tanforan Race Track.*

This picture by Dorothea Lange shows "Civilian Exclusion Order #5," which orders the removal by April 7, 1942, of persons of Japanese ancestry from their homes in San Francisco.

stepped off the bus at his high school. "Instructions to All Persons of JAPANESE Ancestry," the posters stated in cold, black type. "All persons of Japanese ancestry, both alien and non-alien, will be evacuated from the area…" The posters listed dates and times and rules for the evacuation. The rules were clear, blunt, and unavoidable. They were signed by J. L. DeWitt, a lieutenant general in the United States Army. General

Courtesy National Archives, photo no. NWDNS-210-G-C235

Photographer Lange took pictures of Japanese families boarding an evacuation bus in Centerville, California, on May 9, 1942.

Courtesy National Archives, photo no. NWDNS-210-G-C237

DeWitt had been one of the officials charged with solving the so-called "Japanese problem."

If families were not ready to leave their homes in 30 days, the government did not care, Bob Sakata said. And he knew that his family's possessions would be stolen as soon as they left their farm. "We didn't even try to sell our things," he added. "No one would buy them when they could just take them as soon as we were gone. All of your belongings would be gone, no matter what." The Sakatas had no choice but to leave their things behind. "We just left everything we owned," Bob said. "Left everything. Our cars, our trucks, our tractors. Everything." They did manage to keep a few dollars in a savings account.

Throughout the spring of 1942, busses carried away 8,000 Japanese Americans from the San Francisco Bay area. The Sakatas were part of that number. They waited for a bus in Centerville. A well-known photographer named Dorothea Lange recorded their departure on May 9. Her photos show some of the Sakata's 590 neighbors gathering near the Japanese school. The evacuation order put strict limits on what they could take with them. "We were allowed to take only one suitcase each," Bob remembered. The evacuation orders told them to bring their own bed sheets. They were also told to take "knives, forks, spoons, plates, bowls and cups for each member of the family." One rule printed on the evacuation order would have made some children especially sad: "No pets of any kind will be permitted."

Bob Sakata and his family were taken to an assembly center. It was a shocking place. It was not a prison, but it was not a fitting home for families. Many had small children and elderly grandparents. The assembly center was on the grounds of a horse racing track. It was called Tanforan Race Track, near the town of San Bruno south of San Francisco.

When they arrived at Tanforan Race Track, the families were met by soldiers with rifles. The rifles were aimed at the families. The soldiers directed them to registration tables under the grandstand. Their suitcases were searched for **contraband**, such as weapons or cameras. Each person was given a numbered tag to wear. They were treated like convicts going to prison.

Photographer Dorothea Lange had been at Tanforan a few days earlier. She took pictures of the first families arriving there. She was not allowed to photograph the armed soldiers. She was allowed to

Dorothea Lange photographed families arriving at the temporary assembly center at Tanforan RaceTrack on April 29, 1942.

At the Tanforan Race Track, some families were assigned living quarters in the horse stalls shown on the left while others lived in the tar papered barracks on the right.

take photos of the families leaving the grandstand building. One after another, they walk a gravel path onto the race track grounds. It is a sunny day but evidently cool. All of the mothers wear knee-length coats over dresses. Some sport fashionable hats. Some of the fathers are in business suits. The children have been dressed warmly, too. They are in miniature versions of their parents' fashions.

The ones aware of Dorothea's camera are smiling. But their smiles hide some uncertainty, some confusion.

In the photos everyone carries the single suitcase permitted. Some carry travel cases decorated with flower patterns. They look as if they could be going on an exciting vacation. Some hold smaller grips. One teenage boy has only a cardboard box for his clothes. It is tied with string or twine that he uses as a handle. "Palmolive Soap" the box says. He is dressed in jeans and a jean jacket. He could be one of Bob Sakata's high school buddies.

The families were on their way to their assigned rooms, which were located in quickly built, tar-papered **barracks** or in Tanforan's horse stalls. "They gave us each a duffel bag," Bob said, "and then they took us to a straw pile where we put straw in our duffel bag as our mattress. Then they assigned us to a horse stall."

Yoshiko Uchida's family of four was also assigned to a horse stall at Tanforan. Having lived in the city of Berkeley, Yoshiko was appalled when she saw her family's room. She described her experience this way:

When we reached stall number 40, we pushed open the narrow door and looked uneasily into the vacant darkness. The stall was about ten by twenty feet and empty except for three folded

Army cots lying on the floor. Dust, dirt, and wood shavings covered the linoleum that had been laid over manure-covered boards, the smell of horses hung in the air, and the whitened corpses of many insects still clung to the hastily white-washed walls.

Yoshiko Uchida's family — like Bob Sakata's family — would be forced to live in a horse stall at Tanforan for the next five months.

Courtesy National Archives, photo no. NWDNS-210-G-C507

Some of the many children at the assembly center at Tanforan Race Track begged to have their picture taken by photographer Lange in June, 1942.

From our viewpoint today it is obvious that the detention of the Japanese Americans during World War II was cruel and unfair. Yet few of them protested their treatment. It may be difficult for us to understand why they did not. "Our parents came to the United States to look for greener pastures," Bob Sakata said. "I think they were still able to see the potential here, so they kept on telling us to behave. 'Do what the government says and behave.' "

Japanese customs of behavior were very strict. From a young age, children were taught that showing respect for others is vital. Bob Sakata said that respect for others has been handed down from his ancestors. "They were very strict, especially about being respectful of others."

Bob's dad also taught him the value of respecting himself. Everyday Mantaro Sakata said to his children, "Don't ever do anything that will put shame to your name." "That tells it all," Bob said. "That also instilled pride. That's what's lacking in society today."

Respect for others and for self was taught in all Japanese American families. So when the United States government locked them in temporary holding camps like the one at Tanforan, they obeyed. As

Dorothea Lange's photos show, the Japanese Americans smiled and tried to make the best of a bad situation. They obeyed and did not complain. To complain or to protest would have meant to disrespect the authorities and to bring shame on themselves.

Some work had been done to turn the Tanforan Race Track stables into family housing. But the rooms still looked more like horse stalls than apartments. The tops of the wooden doors showed teeth marks where the race horses had chewed on them. The cool breeze blew right into the rooms. The board walls were only horse-high and gave the families little privacy from their neighbors. A single bulb hanging above each room would be their only light. Army cots topped with the straw mattresses would be their only furniture.

Meals for the residents at Tanforan were served in separate buildings. They were called mess halls, which is the army word for cafeteria. The mess halls at Tanforan were always crowded with people eating at wooden picnic tables. Eight hundred people had to be fed in each mess hall. The meals were small and tasted terrible. Beans and bread were the most common foods served. Yoshiko Uchida described her first meal at Tanforan this way:

When I reached the serving table and held out my plate, a cook reached into a dishpan full of canned sausages and dropped two onto my plate with his fingers. Another man gave me a boiled potato and a piece of butterless bread.

Five months later the meals improved slightly. Fried chicken and ice cream were added to Sunday dinners.

Bathrooms and washrooms were in separate buildings. Each section of the camp had men's and women's latrines, another army word. Each latrine had eight toilets but no doors for privacy. The men's and women's washrooms each had one long tin sink lined with faucets. Each washroom had eight showers, but no shower curtains. In addition to this lack of privacy was a frequent lack of hot water. Showering was especially uncomfortable on days when cold, wet winds blew in from the Pacific Ocean just two miles away.

Almost as bad as the dirty and cramped living quarters at Tanforan was the lack of anything to do. Historian Linda Gordon wrote that standing in line was the most common activity. "Lines for breakfast, lines for lunch, lines for supper," she wrote, "lines for

The assembly center at Tanforan Race Track had been open for two days when Dorothea Lange took this picture. The newly arrived evacuees are lining up outside a mess hall for their noon meal. Barracks are shown in the background, and the race track runs diagonally across the picture.

mail, lines for the canteen, lines for laundry tubs, lines for toilets."

Nearly 110,000 Japanese Americans were taken to the temporary assembly centers throughout California, Oregon, and Washington. Settling into small, uncomfortable rooms in the spring of 1942, few could predict what was going to happen to them. Few knew they were settling into the first day of a three-year sentence as prisoners of the United States. Meanwhile their country was fighting for its life against the military forces of Japan.

6 A Dry Spell

During the summer of 1942 the government built ten large **internment** camps. They would replace the assembly centers such as Tanforan. The government would hold the Japanese Americans as prisoners in the camps until the war with Japan was won or lost. So in September, Bob Sakata and the others at Tanforan were displaced again. Again Bob bundled up his straw-filled mattress and his one suitcase. Or maybe he had only a cardboard box. "After five months at Tanforan, they loaded us on an old passenger train," he said. They were transferred to a camp in Utah. It was 450 miles away from their California farm home.

Yoshiko Uchida's family was also taken to Utah in September. She wrote that they were "feeling somewhat like **refugees** carrying our worldly possessions."

They had to file out of Tanforan through two rows of soldiers. "We hurried to the departure point for the inspection of our baggage." Yoshiko guessed that about 500 Tanforan residents boarded the train that day. And it seemed that the rest of the camp had come out to watch them leave.

The train trip lasted two days and nights. It ended in the small farm town of Delta, Utah. There they boarded busses. Through the windows, Yoshiko saw "small farms, cultivated fields, and clusters of trees." Then the pleasant farm land gave way to the white, chalky sand of the Sevier Desert. "The surroundings were now as bleak as a bleached bone," she wrote.

The camp where Yoshiko and Bob were interned was at first called the Central Utah Relocation Center. Someone noticed, however, that the first letters of the words — CURC — could be pronounced "curse." That was not acceptable to government officials. They wanted the camps to have positive-sounding names. The camp was then briefly named for the nearest town. But some Anglo residents demanded that their town name not be linked with a "prison for the innocent." Finally, the name of the camp was changed to Topaz Relocation Center. The name came from

Topaz Mountain, which overlooked the camp from nine miles away.

Topaz is also the name of a gemstone. The front page of a newsletter given to the new residents showed a drawing of a topaz gem. In large print was a headline: "Topaz — Jewel of the Desert." But the Topaz Relocation Center was no jewel. It was even more of a prison than Tanforan had been. Topaz sat on a dry

Courtesy National Archives, photo no. NWDNS-210-G-E011

Bob Sakata and his family were moved with other Japanese Americans from California to the Topaz Internment Camp near Delta, Utah.

desert plain. Snowcapped mountains in the distance were beautiful but gave little comfort. Since the elevation of the camp was nearly a mile high, temperatures could range from a chilly 30° in the morning to a scorching 90° by late afternoon. To cope with that kind of change, the camp residents sometimes needed both winter and summer clothes on the same day.

"[The government] took us to Utah and said it was for our own safety," Bob Sakata said. "When we got to the entrance of the camp, the first thing I noticed as a 16-year-old kid was the [army] sentries on the four corners of the camp." It is easy to see that a teenager like Bob would notice armed soldiers in uniform. It is also easy to see that he could not understand "why the guns were facing in at us instead of out at the world." Bob added, "The thing that I noticed was that their guns were positioned inside, not outside protecting us." The Japanese American families were still considered a threat. Yet they had shown only respect and patience for five months at Tanforan.

The teenage Bob Sakata did not protest to the guards about their guns. Quite the opposite. "That's when I kept my mouth shut," Bob said, "because I didn't want to get in trouble with Dad." But their presence did spark Bob's creativity. "Right away I started to look for every legal way to get out of the camp," he said. There were legal ways to leave Topaz. Bob and his brother Harry would be some of the first to find their way out.

When Yoshiko Uchida's family entered the front gate at Topaz, they were greeted by the music of a Boy Scout drum and bugle corps. The boys were from families that had arrived earlier. As the Scouts marched, she wrote, they became covered with desert dust.

Bob Sakata may have been greeted by the same dusty bugle corps. Certainly he saw dust storms hit Topaz. "[Wind] swept around us in great thrusting gusts," Yoshiko wrote about one storm, "flinging swirling masses of sand in the air and engulfing us in a thick cloud that eclipsed barracks only ten feet away." Pictures of Topaz give hints about just how dusty the camp was. The buildings sit right on the bare, desert sand. There are no lawns. The streets are not paved. In rain or snow, the camp would become a huge mud puddle.

The Topaz camp was a square, one mile on each side. The square was divided into 42 blocks. Each block contained 12 barracks buildings, for about 250 people. Each barrack was 100 feet in length and divided into six rooms. Each room was to house an entire family. At the center of each block were a washroom-latrine building and a laundry. Buildings were only 10 feet apart. So again at Topaz, people would have little

Courtesy National Archives, photo no. NWDNS-210-G-B295

A Boy Scout drum and bugle corps greeted evacuees when they arrived at the Topaz Internment Camp.

privacy. And at Topaz there were a lot of people. In fact, the 8,000 internees forced to live there made the camp Utah's fifth largest city.

In the northeast corner of the camp were the army's headquarters building and a hospital. Around the outside of the camp ran a barbed wire fence. The guard towers that Bob had noticed stood above the four corners.

Most of the barrack rooms were only 20 feet by 18 feet. That is a bit larger than the typical living room today, but each room served as both living room and bedroom for an entire family. Most rooms at Topaz had not even been finished yet. In many barracks "hammering, tarring, and roofing were still in progress," according to Yoshiko Uchida. She also pointed out that "the toilets had no seats, there was no water in the laundry, and the lights didn't work in the showers or latrines... Once again, the Army had sent Japanese Americans into crude, incomplete, and ill-prepared camps."

As was true at Tanforan, the Topaz internees were controlled by government rules and restraints. But Bob Sakata has praised the Japanese adults at Topaz. They did everything possible inside the fences to make life bearable. Living at Topaz would be hard. At least the camp community could be organized. "You gotta hand it to our parents," Bob said. "The first thing they did was organize the blocks...and pick leaders within the blocks. That's the first thing they did. And the second thing they did was form schools. Right away! They recruited anybody who had been to college, and they picked them as teachers. The third thing they did was form churches."

The elected representatives from each block served on a council. They had no real authority, but at least the council fostered communication among the internees and with the authorities. The government "did nothing" about providing education, Bob said. It was only the internees' efforts that assured a continuing education for their children. Regarding churches, the internees practiced the freedom of religion guaranteed in the U.S. Constitution. Membership in a church was one's own choice. According to one source, about 60 percent of the internees were Christian; 40 percent were **Buddhist,** the religion of their ancestry in Japan.

Bob Sakata said that this immediate organization of the internees at Topaz shows a great deal about his people. They valued order and organization, fairness and democracy. They felt personally responsible for their community. And they cherished their religious freedoms. All in all, their values were the values of all other Americans. Unfortunately, for the length of World War II they would not be granted their basic American rights.

Yoshiko Uchida and her sister Keiko — who were college students before the internment — had formed a nursery school during their time at Tanforan Race Track. At Topaz, teachers were given two buildings to use as elementary schools. The classrooms were too small and unfurnished like the living quarters. Parents helped make the rooms as cheerful as possible. One of the teachers in the camp's Mountain View School was Lillian Yamauchi. Miss Yamauchi taught a class of third graders. Every morning she held a discussion with her students about the things that were on their minds. She also encouraged her students to write a daily class diary.

Educational games were part of the activities organized for the children in the nursery school at Topaz Camp.

What her third graders chose to write about gives a kids'-eye view of life in the Topaz camp. On March 11, 1943, the class recorded the following problem that was a common one at Topaz: "Blocks 3, 16, 22, 23 had no running water this morning because the water pipe broke at the high school ground. The people in these blocks went to other places to wash their faces and brush their teeth." On a positive note, the class wrote, "Yesterday we started to join the American Junior Red Cross." The Red Cross is an organization that helps people in times of trouble. Even in their own times of trouble, the youngest Japanese Americans were thinking of helping others.

High school classes were started in a separate building at Topaz. Some students complained that the classes were not as challenging as those they were used to. Sports and other activities were also offered. There was a high school yearbook and a number of clubs, including the Future Farmers of America. Many of the *nisei* had lived on farms in California, so the Topaz High School FFA chapter was popular. By 1943 it had 150 members. Bob Sakata chose not to join. He had other plans.

The Sakatas had arrived at the Topaz camp in

Courtesy National Archives, photo no. NWDNS-210-G-G365

The Topaz High School football team scored the first touchdown in a game with Filmore High School on November 11, 1943. The field at the Topaz camp was sand, not grass.

September of 1942. By December, creative as always, Bob and Harry found their way out. Harry was the first internee at Topaz permitted to work outside the camp. He worked in the beet fields of Idaho summer and fall. Bob was the third internee to leave. He had written to the FFA teacher he had known back in California. He would remember Bob's reputation as a hard worker. The teacher had moved to Fort Collins, Colorado, where he headed the agriculture program at Colorado Agricultural College. The college is now Colorado State University. The teacher's help for Bob came in the form of a letter. It gave Bob a citizen's endorsement. "Somebody had to know you well and write a letter [in your support]," Bob said. "He would be responsible for you, even if you did wrong." The letter was accepted by the government authorities at Topaz.

At age 16, Bob Sakata walked past the armed guards at Topaz again. This time on his way out the front gate. He headed to Brighton, Colorado, where he would earn what money he could to help his family. In the meantime, father Mantaro and sisters Mitsie and Fusi stayed behind the barbed wire fence of Topaz.

During the terrible months of internment, Mantaro Sakata often told his children: "You behave

Know More!

Amache Internment Camp

One internment camp for Japanese Americans was built in Colorado during World War II. It was called the Amache Camp. It was built on the dry plains in the southeast corner of the state near the town of Granada. At Amache there were schools for the children as there were at Topaz and other camps. Internees were allowed to shop in town, and some did farm work in the area.

The Amache Camp opened in August of 1942. At one point it housed 7,318 people. The camp officially closed October 15, 1945.

and you do what the government tells you to do, and you prove that you could be worthy of being an American citizen." Bob thought that was great wisdom. How does Bob Sakata feel today about his imprisonment? "I would describe that total experience as a blessing in disguise," he said graciously. "Because from every hardship, you learn. From every challenge, you learn."

7 Transplanted Again

Bob Sakata was released from Topaz in December, 1942. It had been a year of frustration and fear since the Pearl Harbor attack. Bob crossed over the Rocky Mountains and down to Brighton, Colorado. Brighton was a farm town 20 miles north of Denver. Farmers there raised dairy cows and grew cabbage and sugar beets. Though far from his California home, Brighton must have seemed familiar. Like Centerville where he grew up, Brighton was surrounded by rich farmland. Like Centerville, Brighton had a view of mountains. It may also have reminded him of his father's descriptions of Kurume, Japan. It was also a farm village nestled below mountains.

There were practical reasons why Bob chose to move to Brighton. First, he had personal connections.

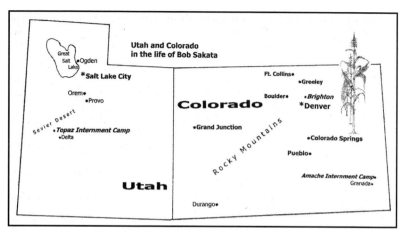

Released in 1942 from the Topaz Internment Camp in Utah, Bob Sakata moved to Brighton, Colorado.

An uncle lived there. Japanese Americans had farmed along the South Platte River since the 1880s. In 1920 they had formed a club called the Brighton Japanese Association to promote good relationships with their Anglo neighbors. Japanese Americans had formed a Buddhist church in Brighton in 1922. By 1924, 84 Japanese immigrants, *issei*, lived in the area. In the 1940s, however, most folks of Japanese descent in Colorado were native born Americans. Nevertheless, after the Pearl Harbor attack anti-Japanese feelings were strong. Those feelings even prompted the Brighton Japanese Association to stop meeting.

There was a second reason Bob chose to move to Colorado. "I had read about Governor Carr," Bob said. Ralph Carr was the governor of Colorado during World War II. He was the only U. S. governor to show fairness toward the Japanese Americans. Governor Carr made a major speech on Colorado radio stations just a few days after the Pearl Harbor attack. He tried to calm the fears and lessen the hatred of Colorado citizens toward the Japanese Americans. The governor asked that people treat them fairly. He made an urgent request that they not say or do anything to embarrass them. They are "truly American," the governor said, whether by birth or immigration. He pointed out that they were as generous with their patriotism "as you and I."

Most importantly for Bob, Governor Carr welcomed the Japanese Americans to Colorado. He saw

that their rights as Americans were about to be taken away. During the first months after the Pearl Harbor attack, the Japanese on the West Coast were still free to move inland. Many accepted the governor's welcome.

Colorado Governor Carr supported the rights of Japanese Americans

Governor Carr also saw that Colorado farmers would soon need extra help.

A shortage of farm workers was developing because so many young men were being drafted into the armed forces. Japanese American farmers from the West Coast could be a big help to Colorado farmers.

It is important to remember that many Americans felt real fear and hatred of the Japanese. Coloradans were no different. Four Colorado farmers in Weld County, north of Brighton, issued an angry statement. They said bluntly that they wanted to "keep California Japs out of Colorado." They did not see why the government should draft farm boys and "replace them with enemy aliens."

One American-born Japanese man living in Brighton was Thomas Kido. He expressed his own strong feelings to Governor Carr. "In peaceful times we were called fine people, fine Americans," Kido said in a letter. "In wartime we are now called…a suspicious, traitorous, and dangerous element." Then Thomas Kido asked, "Must we have white faces to be Americans at all times? "

By chance, during World War II the government used a former canning factory in Brighton as one site to keep German soldiers captured in battle in Europe. They were kept as prisoners of war. They were even put to work harvesting the sugar beet crops around Brighton. The Japanese Americans at Topaz and other internment camps considered themselves prisoners of war, too. But they had never fought against the United States.

In his speech in December of 1941, Governor Carr urged his Colorado listeners to "remember that America is the great melting pot of the modern civilized world. From every nation of the globe people have come to the United States who sought to live as free men…" In many other speeches Carr made this argument clearly: "We must preserve the rights of all men under the Constitution." Bob Sakata read about Governor Carr's beliefs. In December of 1942, he accepted his invitation.

In Brighton, Bob stayed with his uncle for a short time. Then he went to work for Bill Schluter. He was to be yet another positive influence in the life of Bob Sakata. Bill Schluter was an older man who needed help on his dairy farm. Bob did farm chores for him and milked his cows. In return, Schluter fed Bob and allowed him to sleep on a cot in his concrete milk house. It was no more comfortable than the rooms Bob had lived in at Tanforan and Topaz. On the farm, though, he was free to work. He was also free to finish high school.

Bob had not stayed at Topaz long enough to take classes at the camp's school. Yet, he was determined to earn his high school diploma in Colorado. As soon as possible, he enrolled at Brighton High School. One morning during a class, Bob was called to the principal's office. His first reaction as "Oh man, what did I do wrong?" Principal Dave Kyle invited Bob into his office. "Sit down," Mr. Kyle said, making Bob a bit nervous. "Tell me, Robert," Mr. Kyle began, "why do you want to go to school?" The question surprised Bob. But he had a ready answer. Bob said, "Mr. Kyle, I need an education. Why do you ask, sir?" Mr. Kyle's response surprised Bob again. Mr. Kyle said, "Robert, you have a lot more credits than we require for graduation." Bob's records from his California school had arrived. They showed the extra classes Bob had taken there. In two years, he had taken as many classes as most students do in three.

Mr. Kyle smiled. "I could give you a diploma today," he said. Bob could have accepted Mr. Kyle's offer. He could have gotten out of school right then. A less-motivated student would have jumped at the offer. Not Bob. Getting out of high school did not fit his plan to enroll at Colorado Agricultural College. Bob politely said, "Thank you, Mr. Kyle, but my wish is to enter [college] as a major in **agronomy**. So I need more chemistry and math." With the high school diploma that Mr. Kyle offered him, Bob might have been able to go to college. But Bob was more concerned about being well prepared. Mr. Kyle allowed Bob to finish his classes at Brighton High School. That year Bob also brushed up on math subjects such as algebra, geometry, and trigonometry.

Then Bob found time for some fun. And he showed off a different kind of creativity. In the spring of 1943, Bob joined a band. He played the drums. The band practiced in the school auditorium during lunch periods. The other students at the school were excited to hear them play. Maybe too excited. An article in the student newspaper, The *Brightonian*, made this plea: "The band wishes to stress that no one is admitted into the auditorium during the rehearsals at noon." The band, which had no name, played for Friday afternoon socials at the school in May. They even played for the school's prom that spring. The student newspaper compared Bob Sakata to the most popular jazz drummer of the 1940s, Gene Krupa. "Gene Krupa, the wicked drummer, has been taking lessons from that new sensation, [drum] beatin' Bob Sakata," one of his classmates wrote. Bob was called "the leader of the 'keeps ya guessin' rhythms."

Bob was one of many new students in Brighton in 1942 while the fighting against Japan and Germany was raging. A dozen or more Japanese American teenagers had moved from California. Like Bob, some may have spent time in government camps. Did they feel discrimination because of their race? Hisa Horiuchi remembered being discriminated against in Brighton during World War II. And Hisa had lived in Brighton since birth. In an interview she added that she was never really bullied. "War is hate," she said, "and when war is over, hate is gone."

After the Pearl Harbor attack, some at Brighton High were accusing the Japanese students of favoring Japan in the war. The student editors of the *Brightonian* wrote that those accusations had "absolutely no justification." They challenged their Anglo classmates with the following words:

Remember that the Japanese in this school are as good Americans as any of us…and it is wrong to make them feel like outcasts. So let us take this as a gentle reminder that we young people are here to learn — to learn that the only worthwhile and successful aim is to make this a better democratic world for ALL people.

During the 1940s, Americans found many ways to help the country win the war. Students helped, too. For just a few pennies they could buy government defense stamps. The money raised by the stamps bought supplies for the troops. Americans also collected scrap metal and rubber that was recycled into everything from bullets to battleships.

President Roosevelt gave a speech in which he suggested another way for students to serve their country. He said that high school students could best serve by helping farmers harvest their important crops. Nature was good to farmers in the winter of 1941 - 1942. She dumped much snow on Colorado. The moisture would produce a bigger crop than normal. The big crop meant that farmers needed even more help. In the fall, students at Brighton High were given two days off of school to harvest sugar beets. The *Brightonian* said, "A good percentage of the students answered the call to the fields..." Without the extra help, farmers would have lost much of their crop. Sugar beets left in the ground would have rotted.

In November, 1942, Ralph Carr ran again for governor. Many people in Colorado were still upset that he had welcomed the Japanese Americans to the state. Voters did not reelect him.

In June, 1943, Bob Sakata graduated from Brighton High School. His father, brother, and sisters were still being held in Utah.

8 Harvest

Small towns are like families. Small town people care for each other, but sometimes they squabble. In January, 1944, a group of Brighton farmers and businessmen were angry. So was the mayor. They were angry that so many Japanese Americans were buying farms and businesses. They wanted to make it illegal for aliens to do so. They even pushed the issue all the way to a state-wide vote. Surprisingly, Colorado voters disagreed with the angry Brighton men. Japanese Americans kept the right to buy land.

Brighton farmer Bill Schluter saw no problem with Japanese Americans owning land. He asked Bob Sakata if his family would like to buy a farm. "Yes!" Bob said. But they did not have enough money saved to buy one. In the spring Bill Schluter stepped up.

Years later journalist Bill Hosokawa wrote about Bill Schluter's generosity:

> ...Schluter sat Bob down and said something like: "Tell your folks to come out of the camp. I've just bought you a farm — 40 acres with good water rights here on the outskirts of Brighton. The price is $6,000 — $150 dollars an acre — and you can pay me back whenever you can."

Bill Schluter's generosity made the year 1944 a turning point in the Sakatas' lives. Mantaro, Harry, Mitsie, and Fusi were allowed to leave Topaz. They joined Bob in Brighton on land that would be their own. They moved into a house on the farm. It was small. It had no plumbing for running water, but it was livable. The reunited Sakata family would farm again.

New farm equipment was expensive. "We just started with a team of horses and a used John Deere tractor," Bob said. Before planting crops they needed a piece of equipment called a leveler. Again, Bob got creative. "I built [a leveler] with railroad ties and timbers," he said. His leveler had to be adjusted by hand, unlike today's equipment. Sugar beets had been grown

Know More!

The Fiery End of World War II

In 1945 the United States and its allies won the war in Europe. Germany surrendered on May 8. In the Pacific war, the United States troops had pushed the Japanese forces all the way back to Japan. At that point, the only way to defeat them was to invade their country. But that would have meant even more deadly fighting. Instead, President Harry S. Truman decided to use a new, highly secret weapon against Japan: the atomic bomb. On August 6, the United States dropped the world's first atomic bomb on the city of Hiroshima, Japan. The bomb killed 40,000 people instantly. Hiroshima is 150 miles northeast of Kurume, Mantaro Sakata's boyhood village. Three days later, another atomic bomb was dropped even closer to Kurume. The second bomb's target was the city of Nagasaki, just 50 miles to the southwest. The two huge bombs stopped Japan from fighting further. Japan surrendered to the United States on August 14, 1945. World War II came to an end.

After the Pearl Harbor attack, many Americans had feared that the *issei* and *nisei* would become traitors to the United States. None did. Just the opposite happened. Many of the nisei generation volunteered for military service, even those who had been imprisoned in the camps. Most of the volunteers were placed in an army unit called the 442nd Regimental Combat Team. The 442nd fought remarkably hard. Many of them were killed in Europe fighting for their country. They fought so bravely that the 442nd became the most honored combat unit in U.S. military history.

The end of World War II was a great relief for all Americans. For the Japanese Americans still in the internment camps, the war's end was also a return to freedom.

The Topaz internment camp was closed forever on October 31, 1945.

on the land. Bob, Harry, and their dad planted vegetables instead. They grew lettuce, cabbage, tomatoes, cucumbers, onions, and green beans. Their farm was so productive they were able to pay for it completely in just two years. For the first time the Sakatas owned a piece of America.

American farmers had always used barnyard manure to fertilize crops. Manure was readily available and organic. But it was the same type of fertilizer Mantaro Sakata had used in Japan in the 1880s. His sons began to use newly developed chemical fertilizers and **herbicides**. These products helped their crops grow bigger and better. When Bob started farming in 1944, 26 percent of the population in the United States was farmers. "It took 26 percent of us to grow the food for everybody [in America]," he said. Today less than two percent of our population farms. American farmers also feed much of the rest of the world. Technology has made farming that much more efficient, Bob said. Today, however, some farmers are changing their methods again. Some use fewer chemical fertilizers. Some have stopped using them completely.

In 1944 Harry Sakata again trucked vegetables to market, this time Denver's Denargo Market. Bob made time to study agronomy and **horticulture**. He took university extension classes in Brighton. Bob said, "I wanted to learn."

Starting in 1949 Bob faced a whole new set of challenges.

His dad was dreaming about Japan. Mantaro had not been back to the village of Kurume in 50 years. He wanted to see his brothers again. Bob drove his dad to California to apply for a passport needed for the trip. Returning to Colorado they were involved in a traffic accident in New Mexico. Mantaro and another passenger in the car were killed. Mantaro's dream would not be fulfilled. Bob was badly injured. He was transferred to a hospital in Denver to recover. "That was a low point in my life," Bob said. "It was emotionally and mentally tough, because I was driving when the crash happened."

In 1951 another accident almost killed Bob. In his shop early one morning he lit a gas torch to weld a piece of equipment. Something went wrong and the gas exploded. Flames roared up Bob's legs. Over half of his body was terribly burned. An ambulance rushed him to the local hospital. Nurses in the emergency room thought he was dead. "They covered me with a

The Sakata family was reunited in Brighton, Colorado, in 1944. The men in the family posed for this portrait soon afterward. From the left: Bob, Mantaro and Harry Sakata.

white sheet," Bob said.

Then his family doctor arrived. "He just chewed everybody out," Bob said. The doctor was upset that they were not working to save Bob's life. "You don't know this guy," the doctor said. "Take him to surgery. Quick!"

In the operating room Bob heard doctors talking, but he was unable to speak. "This guy can't feel a thing," one said. He assumed that the feeling in Bob's legs had been destroyed. He started working without putting Bob to sleep with anesthesia. "They were tearing my coveralls off and pruning out all the burnt skin," Bob said. A nurse holding his hand said, "He's feeling everything you're doing." The doctor asked how she knew that. "He's about ready to break my wrist," she answered. His will to live was strong.

Bob spent a year as a burn patient at University Hospital in Denver. Doctors there thought he would no longer be able to walk. But his will to walk again was as strong as his will to live. "That's when I learned that there is an Almighty," Bob said. He thanked his doctors for their work, but he told them, "Why don't you let me and my God figure out whether I can walk again." The pain was awful, but in time Bob did walk.

After his accidents, Bob began a spiritual search. He wanted to join a church. He visited every one in Brighton. Standing for prayers and hymns was painful because he had to wear leg braces and walk with canes. Then Bob was invited to the Presbyterian Church. When he stood during the Presbyterian service, there was no pain. He said to himself, "This is the church I'm going to belong to." He has been a member ever since.

Many individuals have affected Bob's life. In return he has affected others' lives. One of them was Felix Garcia. He was the surgeon who treated Bob's burns during his year at University Hospital. When Dr. Garcia retired 26 years later, he still remembered Bob. In a letter, Dr. Garcia praised Bob's spirit. He wrote that Bob's spirit had helped him "conquer all the terrible mental, emotional, and physical damage that is part of a major burn."

Bob faced a third challenge when his brother Harry became ill. Harry had always been healthy and "husky as a mule," Bob said. In 1955 he was being treated at a Denver hospital but was not improving. One day Bob had a strong feeling that he must visit Harry. Some would say "an inner voice" told him he had to see Harry immediately.

Doctors had kept the cause of Harry's illness a secret. Somehow Bob knew it was cancer. After a short talk with Harry, Bob asked if he could say a prayer. Harry said yes. Bob prayed, "Dear Lord, if you love him more than I do, take him now." The prayer told Harry that his brother knew how serious the illness was. Harry took Bob's hand. "How did you know that I had cancer?" Harry asked. The brothers then had a heart-to-heart talk. They talked about everything that had happened in their lives, and they talked about what would happen to the farm.

Bob called his sisters, who had moved back to California. They hurried to Denver and had their own heart-to-heart talk with Harry. Harry passed away the very next morning. He was only 35 years old. Bob called his last talk with Harry a "miracle conversation." If he had not followed his "inner voice," Bob would have missed the opportunity to talk with Harry one last time.

The farm was now in Bob's hands. His faith helped him deal with his losses. He learned from those losses that "without faith in God there is no meaning or purpose in life." The next year was a much happier one. Bob had fallen in love. In 1956 he married

Joanna Tokunaga. She was one of Bob's neighbors. Her father had also emigrated from Japan to farm in Colorado. With Joanna, Bob moved on to the next chapter of his life.

9 Back to the Roots

For 40 years Bob expanded Sakata Farms. His small farm became a big business. By the 1990s he owned 3,000 acres along the South Platte River. His fields stretch north from Brighton for 20 miles. He grew the vegetables most in demand in supermarkets, especially corn and onions. He adapted machinery to make his farming more efficient. Plus, he always made time to help others.

People from around the world began to recognize Bob Sakata's accomplishments, even the Emperor of Japan.

The emperor of Japan rarely leaves his Imperial Palace. But in 1994 he made a 20-day tour of the United States. One of the places he wanted to see in Colorado was Sakata Farms. Bob and Joanna Sakata were to be visited by royalty, Emperor Akihito and his wife, Empress Michiko.

Anyone who meets the emperor must follow strict rules called **protocols**. Following these rules shows courtesy and respect. Bob definitely wanted to be respectful. He asked the Japanese ambassador to coach him. Some of the protocols were easy to remember. "If the emperor extends his hand for a handshake," the ambassador said, "you may shake his hand. If the emperor does not give you his hand, you must simply

Photograph courtesy of Bob Sakata

In 1994, the Emperor and Empress of Japan paid a visit to Colorado and to Sakata Farms. Here, they are speaking with Joanna Sakata, left.

*Bob Sakata, right, shows Sakata Farms' produce to
Emperor Akihito and Empress Michiko.*

bow to him." Other protocols were a bit puzzling. The Japanese ambassador told Bob, "Never speak directly to the emperor. Speak only to his interpreter." This is a protocol that must be followed, even though the emperor understands English quite well.

Emperor Akihito wanted to see an American farmer at work. It had been a dry spring. On the morning the emperor arrived in Brighton, however, it was raining. The rain made the Sakatas more nervous about the imperial visit than they had already been. The emperor arrived at their home in a limousine. Just as the door was opened for the emperor, the rain stopped. Bob was so excited that he forgot all he had learned about protocol. He walked right up to the emperor and extended his hand. The emperor evidently forgot protocol, too. He returned Bob's handshake. "My father always said the emperor was a god," Bob blurted. "You must be. You made the rain stop!" Bob had broken the protocols.

Luckily, the Emperor of Japan was equally excited to meet Bob Sakata. They began speaking like old friends. They spoke in English, but Bob also attempted some "broken Japanese." It was an historic moment. The Emperor of Japan was talking directly with the son of a poor Japanese farmer. It was a conversation between His Imperial Majesty and the son of the lowly "honey pot" carrier.

The emperor and his empress were seated near an eight-acre field. The field had been left bare by Bob's staff. They had prepared an impressive show. Journalist Bill Hosokawa remembered it well. "Lined up on the field," he wrote, "were about a dozen pieces of farm equipment including a number of huge tractors." The staff showed how with modern equipment the bare field could be "plowed, harrowed, smoothed, and made ready for planting within thirty minutes." According to Bill Hosokawa, "It was an impressive display of harnessed horsepower unfamiliar to the Japanese." The emperor was then invited to climb into the cab of one huge tractor. He fiddled with levers as Bob explained how the tractor worked.

During his visit, the emperor asked Bob a key question. In Japanese, he asked, "How did someone who was so mistreated by his government go on to be so successful?" The emperor was referring to Bob's time in the Tanforan and Topaz internment camps. Bob answered that mistreatment can always be corrected in a democracy like ours. And success is possi-

Know More!

Japanese Emperors During the Lives of the Sakata Family

The position of emperor is passed from father to son. There have been only four emperors since Mantaro Sakata was born in Japan in 1884. The emperor is never called by his personal name. That would be thought too familiar, even an insult. In Japan the emperor must be called "His Imperial Majesty the Emperor" or "His Imperial Majesty."

The emperor lives in Edo Castle in central Tokyo. The castle is protected by high walls and a moat. The emperor lives a very private life. He appears before his citizens only twice a year.

Emperor Meiji reigned from 1867 to 1912. His personal name was Mutsuhito.

Mantaro Sakata grew up during Emperor Meiji's reign. Like other Japanese citizens, Mantaro considered the emperor a god.

Emperor Taishÿ reigned from 1912 to 1926. His personal name was Yoshihito.

He died the year Bob Sakata was born.

Emperor Shÿwa reigned from 1926 to 1989. His personal name was Hirohito.

Pearl Harbor was attacked during his reign on December 7, 1941. Emperor Shÿwa, Hirohito, surrendered to the United States on August 14, 1945, which ended World War II.

His Imperial Majesty began his reign in 1989. His personal name is Akihito.

He is the current emperor. He is the 125th emperor in Japan's long history and the only world leader with the title "emperor." His Imperial Majesty, Emperor Akihito, visited Colorado and Bob Sakata's farm in 1994.

ble for anyone living under our **free enterprise system**. To succeed, Bob always says, a person must "work harder and think smarter." Bob's successful life is a perfect example of what makes America great.

On his last day in Colorado, the emperor attended a farewell luncheon. It was hosted by Governor Roy Romer. When the emperor spoke he praised Ralph Carr, the former governor who had welcomed Japanese Americans to Colorado in 1942. Then the emperor broke protocol again. He spoke about his country's past. And he apologized for the hardships Japan had caused during World War II. This must have been difficult for him to do. Emperor Akihito's own father had been emperor during the war. Bob Sakata said that it was a real "tear-jerker moment." Rarely had the Emperor of Japan spoken his feelings so openly.

In 2004, Bob and Joanna Sakata spoke with the emperor again. This time they visited his home, the Imperial Palace in Tokyo, Japan. Bob also visited Kurume, the home Mantaro Sakata had left 102 years earlier. Kurume had grown from a village to a large city. Fruits and vegetables are still raised in Kurume but mostly in greenhouses.

In Kurume, Bob spoke to members of the Japanese American Society. "It is amazing how the world has changed even in my lifetime," he said. It is amazing. In his lifetime Bob Sakata has gone from poverty and imprisonment to success and respect. Referring to World War II, Bob went on with his speech. "Sixty years ago you Japanese were enemies of us Americans. Today we are allies; working together to keep peace in the world, to raise the living standards of less fortunate nations, and to promote understanding that knows no barriers."

Bob and Joanna raised a family during their busy lives in Brighton, Colorado. They have two daughters, Vicki and Lani. The have a son named Robert. "Pretty soon my son will be taking over," Bob said. "But I'm still glad to have Sakata Farms in the Brighton community." Robert, too, will deal with problems. Water for crops is always in short supply in Colorado. New houses continue to crowd out farmland. Fewer workers are available to do the hands-on work needed to weed and harvest vegetables. But like his father, Robert will find creative solutions. It's the American way.

Bob Sakata's Philosophy of Life

Ten Simple "Don'ts" I Try to Live by
by Bob Sakata

Don't just look, *observe.*

Don't just hear, *listen.*

Don't just talk, *say something.*

Don't just work, *be productive.*

Don't just set goals, *achieve them.*

Don't just live on a title, *continue to prove you are worthy of it.*

Don't just tell the truth, *live it.*

Don't just love, *have respect and honor with it.*

Don't just make a promise, *follow through with it.*

Don't just pray, *have faith.*

Timeline

1884 — Mantaro Sakata born in Kurume, Japan.

1902 — Mantaro Sakata immigrates to San Francisco.

1906 — Earthquake and fire destroy San Francisco.

1920 — Mantaro Sakata marries his "picture bride," Aki Nishimura.

1926 — Bob Sakata born in San Jose, California.

1941 — Japan attacks U. S. Navy at Pearl Harbor, Hawaii, on December 7, with the permission of Emperor Hirohito.

1942 — President Franklin Roosevelt issues Executive Order 9066. More than 110,000 Japanese Americans sent to internment camps in seven Western states. Sakata family sent first to Tanforan Race Track, San Bruno, California, then Topaz Internment Camp in Utah. In December, Bob Sakata leaves Topaz for Brighton, Colorado.

1943 — Bob Sakata graduates from Brighton High School.

1944 — The Sakata family begins farming again on land bought from Bill Schluter.

1945 — President Franklin Roosevelt dies. Harry S. Truman becomes president. The U.S. drops atomic bombs on Hiroshima and Nagasaki, Japan, ending World War II.

1949 — Mantaro Sakata dies in a car accident in New Mexico.

1951 — Bob Sakata seriously burned in shop fire.

1955 — Harry Sakata dies of cancer, leaving the Brighton farm to his brother Bob.

1956 — Bob Sakata marries Joanna Tokunaga.

1989 — Japanese Emperor Hirohito dies. His son, Akihito, becomes emperor.

1994 — Japanese Emperor Akihito visits Colorado.

New Words

acre — a measure of land; 43,560 square feet

agronomy — the science and economics of crop production

alien — a foreign-born resident who is not a citizen

antibiotic — a medicine that treats infectious diseases

barrack — a building used to house soldiers or workers

bilingual — able to speak two different languages

Buddhist — a person who follows the religion and thinking of Buddha

columnist — a person who writes for a newspaper and expresses opinions

contraband — anything not allowed by law

discrimination — unfair treatment against someone, usually because of race

elder — an older person; a parent or grandparent

emigrate — to leave one's country

entrepreneur — a person who starts and runs a business

evacuation — the removal of people from their home area

fertilizer — a material placed in soil to improve plant growth

free enterprise — the freedom to own a business without government interference

herbicide — a chemical that destroys plants, usually weeds

horticulture — the art or science of growing plants

immigrant — a person who enters a new country to live there

internment — being held as a prisoner

interpreter — a person who helps people communicate when they speak different languages

issei — (*EES say*) a first generation Japanese immigrant to America

nisei — (*KNEE say*) an American-born son or daughter of a Japanese immigrant

penicillin — a medicine used to treat infections

pneumonia — (*new MOAN yah*) an infection in the lungs

prejudice — an opinion held without considering facts

protocol — a set of rules for proper and respectful behavior

refugee — a person who flees home for protection, usually in a time of war

Sources

Brighton (Colo.) *Brighton Blade*, 1950.

Brighton (Colo.) *Brightonian*, 1941, 1942, 1943, 2006.

Dorr, W. Carl. *Looking Back: A Historical Account of the Development of Brighton and Surrounding Community from 1859 - 1976.* Brighton Centennial Commission, 1976.

Frandsen, Maude Linstrom. *All the Way: An Account of the Development of a City and a Church.* Self-published, No Date.

Gordon, Linda and Gary Y. Okihiro, eds. *Impounded: Dorothea Lange and the Censored Images of Japanese American Internment.* New York: W.W. Norton & Company, Inc., 2006.

Hane, Mikiso. *Peasants, Rebels, and Outcasts: The Underside of Modern Japan.* New York: Pantheon Books, 1982.

History of Brighton, Colorado and Surrounding Area. Brighton, CO: Brighton Historic Preservation Commission, 2006.

Hosokawa, Bill. *Colorado's Japanese Americans from 1886 to the Present.* Boulder, CO: University Press of Colorado, 2005.

— *Nisei: The Quiet Americans.* Niwot, CO: University Press of Colorado, 1992.

Lamar, Howard R., ed. *The New Encyclopedia of the American West.* New Haven: Yale University Press, 1998.

Manchester, William. *The Glory and the Dream: A Narrative History of America, 1932-1972.* vol. 1 Boston: Little, Brown and Company, 1973.

Perez, Louis G. *Daily Life in Early Modern Japan.* Westport, CT: Greenwood Press, 2002.

Schrager, Adam. *The Principled Politician: The Ralph Carr Story.* Golden, CO: Fulcrum Publishing, 2008.

Stanley, Jerry. *I Am an American: A True Story of Japanese Internment.* New York: Scholastic, Inc., 1994. *

Tunnell, Michael O. and George W. Chilcoat, eds. *The Children of Topaz: The Story of the Japanese-American Internment Camp.* New York: Holiday House, 1996. *

Uchida, Yoshiko. *Desert Exile: The Uprooting of a Japanese American Family.* Seattle: University of Washington Press, 1982. *

Way It Was, The. Oral History, 2003. Brighton High School, Brighton, CO.

INTERVIEWS

"21st Century Farming with Bob Sakata." Interview by Hattie Bryant. Small Business School. http://search.smallbusinessschool.org/video.cfm?clip=1521

Sakata, Bob. December 17, 2007; January 7, 2008; May 12, 2008; May 22, 2008; June 4, 2008.

SPEECHES

Sakata, Bob. Address. Japanese American Society meeting. Kurume, Japan, 21 Feb. 2004.

WEB SITES

All Experts. http://en.allexperts.com/q/U-S-History-672/ German-American-population-during.htm

"Amache Japanese Interment Camp, The" Colorado State Archives. http://www.colorado.gov/dpa/archives/wwcod/granada.htm

* For young readers

Beckwith, Jane. "Topaz Camp" http://www.millardcounty.com/topazcamp.html

Club Historian. http://www.clubhistorian.com/

Colorado State University. "Produce Leader is Colorado State's Distinguished Alumni Winner." http://agnews.colostate.edu/index.asp?page=news_item_display&news_item_id=-914456669

Densho. The Japanese American Legacy Project. http://www.densho.org/

Japanese American Relocation Digital Archives. http://www.calisphere.universityofcalifornia.edu/jarda/

Japanese American Veterans Association. "Winning the Purple Heart with the Marines on Iwo - Nobuo Furuiye" http://www.javadc.org/Action%20in%20Pacific.htm

Military Intelligence Service Research Center. "Nobuo Furuiye" http://www.njahs.org/misnorcal/profiles/profile.php?id=1009

National Archives http://arcweb.archives.gov

Reid, T.R. "Feeding the Planet." National Geographic.com http://www.nationalgeographic.com/features/2000/population/planet/body.html

Wikipedia. "Topaz War Relocation Center" http://en.wikipedia.org/wiki/Topaz_War_Relocation_Center

Index

Acknowledgments

I first met Bob Sakata in 1975. I was a struggling young English teacher with only two years of experience, newly hired by the school district in Brighton, Colorado. Bob was president of the school board. Brighton was good to me. I taught there for the next 32 years. I knew of Bob's achievements as a farmer and a business leader. I admired his generous spirit, his work ethic, and his unflinching dedication to American values. It was only during the past few years, however, that I learned of the obstacles that had been thrown Bob's way.

The journalism of Bill Hosokawa and Adam Schrager were most helpful in placing Bob Sakata's story in historical context. Photographs by Dorothea Lange put a human face on that history, as did the memories of Yoshiko Uchida. Articles by amateur journalists — Bob Sakata's classmates in 1941 and 1942 — provided some surprising perspectives. Their observations in their student newspaper, The Brightonian, have been obsessively collected and preserved by Mel Bacon of Brighton. But I am most thankful to Bob Sakata himself for the time he made for our conversations.

About the Author

Daniel Blegen taught English, journalism, speech, and drama at the middle school, high school, and community college levels for 34 years. He has written on the arts for magazines and newspapers. He is also a poet and playwright.Blegen is coauthor, with Melvin Bacon, of *Bent's Fort: Crossroads of Cultures on the Santa Fe Trail*. He lives and writes in Longmont, Colorado.

More Now You Know Bios

Chipeta
1843 – 1924
ISBN 978-0-86541-091-6. $8.95

Mary Elitch Long
1856-1936
ISBN 978-0-86541-094-7. $8.95

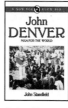

John Denver
1943 – 1997
ISBN 978-086541-088-6. $8.95

Dottie Lamm
ISBN 978-086541-085-5. $8.95

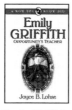

Emily Griffith
1868-1947
ISBN 978-0-86541-077-0. $8.95

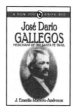

José Dario Gallegos
1830-1883
ISBN 978-0-86541-084-8. $8.95

John Wesley Powell
1834-1902
ISBN 978-0-86541-080-0. $8.95

Justina Ford
1871-1952
ISBN 978-0-86541-074-9. $8.95

Enos Mills
1870-1922
ISBN 978-0-86541-072-5. $8.95

Martha Maxwell
1831-1881
ISBN 978-0-86541-075-6. $8.95

Molly Brown
1867-1932
ISBN 978-0-86541-081-7. $8.95

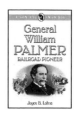

General William Palmer
1836 – 1909
ISBN 978-0-86541-092-3. $8.95

Now You Know Bios are available at your local bookstore,
by calling 888.570.2663, and online at www.FilterPressBooks.com